796.34   6.00

May, Julian

AUTHOR
Forest Hills and the American
TITLE Tennis Championship

Veteran Tennis star Gussie Moran, a sensation in the 1940's, still displays fine form in the Forest Hills tournament 30 years later.

SPORTS CLASSIC

FOREST HILLS & THE AMERICAN TENNIS CHAMPIONSHIP

By JULIAN MAY

Creative Education
Childrens Press

PHOTO CREDITS:

UPI . . . . Cover, 2, 10, 27, 31, 34, 38, 39, 43
FOS, Inc. 26, 29, 37, 40, 44, 46
Steven E. Sutton 1, 18, 32, 33
Acme Photo 14, 16, 17, 22

Published by Creative Educational Society, Inc., 123 South Broad Street,
Mankato, Minnesota 56001. Copyright © 1976 by Creative Educational
Society, Inc. International copyrights reserved in all countries.
No part of this book may be reproduced in any form without written
permission from the publisher. Printed in the United States.

Library of Congress Cataloging in Publication Data
May, Julian.
    Forest Hills and the American tennis championship. (Sports classic)
    SUMMARY: Profiles of some of the outstanding tennis players
who have won at Forest Hills since the United States championships
began there in 1915.
    1. Tennis—Biography—Juvenile literature. 2. Tennis— United
States—History—Juvenile literature. 3. West Side Tennis Club,
Forest Hills, N.Y.—Juvenile literature [1. Tennis—Biography.
2. Tennis—History. 3. West Side Tennis Club, Forest Hills, N.Y.] I. Title.
GV994.A1M37   796.34′2′0922 [B]   [920]   76-4481
ISBN 0-87191-505-7

Contents

The U.S. Championship

A woman, Miss Mary Ewing Outerbridge, first brought tennis to the United States. It happened in 1874. Mary saw British officers playing the new game in Bermuda and brought home tennis equipment to her home in New York.

Within a few years, wealthy people all along the East Coast (and later in California) were batting tennis balls politely back and forth. Tennis courts were built in private clubs, and only the wealthy members could play. This didn't bother the ordinary people much; they thought tennis was a sissy game!

The first men's singles championship match was played in Newport, R.I., in 1881. The winner was Richard Dudley Sears. The first women's match took place in 1887 in Philadelphia and was won by Ellen Hansell.

As interest in tennis grew, the annual championship matches attracted more spectators. The men's event was moved to the West Side Tennis Club of Forest Hills, N.Y., in 1915; while the women's remained in Philadelphia until 1920.

"Forest Hills," as the U.S. championship match came to be called, now attracts hundreds of thousands of fans for its September tournament. Players come from all over the world to play on its courts, knowing that Forest Hills presents one of the greatest challenges in the world of tennis.

Big Bill Tilden

To tell the truth, pioneer tennis was a pretty dull game. Players, dressed in tight-fitting suits or long dresses, skipped sedately over the grass courts. Spectators were supposed to clap discreetly at well-played shots. No wonder the working-class people sneered at the snobbish game!

Just before World War I, however, tennis styles began to change. A Californian named William M. Johnston introduced a bullet-like forehand that brought new excitement to the game. Johnston was only 5 feet 8 inches tall and weighed a frail 120 pounds, but he became one of the greatest volleyers of all time. He won the first Forest Hills championship in 1915.

After serving in World War I, Johnston came back. He faced a newcomer named William Tatem Tilden II in the 1919 championship, and one of the world's great sports rivalries was born. Tilden was tall, 6 feet 2, with a fast, versatile style. When he played against the tiny Johnston at Forest Hills, it was "Big Bill *vs.* Little Bill."

That year, Little Bill won handily — 6-4, 6-4, 6-3. Fans were delighted at Johnston's comeback; but Tilden crept away to rework his game, determined to become the best tennis player in the world.

Bill Tilden was a brooding, intense man with a giant ego and many personal problems; but he was an agile and extremely clever player who could not only analyze and correct his own faults, but also see those of his opponent and exploit them to the fullest. He won Wimbledon in 1920, whipping Australia's "unbeatable" Gerald Patterson and becoming America's first male Wimbledon winner.

Then Tilden returned to the U.S. and took on Little Bill Johnston at Forest Hills in one of tennis' greatest battles.

Tilden won the first set, 6-1; Johnston took the second, 6-1. But in the midst of the third set, a small airplane, flying over the Tennis Club, crashed, narrowly missing the stands! The players paused for a moment, then played on.

The accident was forgotten as the two tennis masters see-sawed back and forth in a match full of suspense and thrills. Tilden won the third set, 7-5; and Johnston won the fourth, 7-5. Normally aloof fans cheered, screamed, and groaned during the tie-breaker. Johnston finally began to falter and drove out at last after a great rally. Tilden won set and match, 6-3.

Big Bill won Forest Hills six times in a row before he went into a slump in 1926. People said he was through, but Tilden's burning pride kept him trying. In 1929, at the age of 37, he made a great comeback and won his seventh U.S. championship at Forest Hills. To cap the triumph, he won at Wimbledon again, too. Tilden went on to become a professional player, a man who squandered two fortunes and made many enemies with his arrogant, quarrelsome personality.

His personal problems faded, however, when he was on the tennis court. There, Big Bill Tilden was one of the greatest.

The West Side Tennis Club at Forest Hills, N.Y.,
site of the annual U.S. Open Tennis Championships.

Empress of the Court

Before women tennis players could become truly outstanding, they had to overcome two big handicaps — the "ladylike" style of play and long dresses!

The first barrier was crashed by sturdy Molla Bjurstedt, a Norwegian girl who came to America on a visit in 1914 and stayed to become Forest Hills' first Queen of the Court. Molla played aggressively with scorching baseline drives. Beginning in 1915, she won the U.S. title four years in a row. Marriage to an American stockbroker named Mallory took her mind off tennis in 1919, and she lost the championship; but she came back in 1920 and won the U.S. women's singles three more times in a row.

Meanwhile, a graceful Frenchwoman disposed of long skirts on the court forever. She was Suzanne Lenglen, agile as a cat, who floated over the tennis courts of Europe in filmy short skirts that caused a sensation. She, too, was called the Queen of Tennis, having won Wimbledon three times between 1919 and 1921.

Suzanne and Molla first played against each other in Paris in 1921. The Frenchwoman won. This encouraged Suzanne to challenge Molla for the American title the following year. Acting the prima donna, oozing confidence, disdain, and Parisian chic, Suzanne arrived at Forest Hills like a movie star and was heavily favored to win.

Husky, homely Molla waded in like a lioness. The Norwegian-American would show them all who was Queen of the Court! She won the first set, 6-2, and swept ahead in the second. Suddenly Lenglen's nerve broke. Weeping, she rushed from the court, declaring that she was ill. Molla Bjurstedt Mallory was U.S. champion for the seventh time.

But her reign was nearly at an end. In 1922, she bowed to Lenglen at Wimbledon; and at Forest Hills, Molla was defeated by a 17-year-old California girl, Helen Wills. Helen's easy victory, 6-2, 6-1, was an omen of things to come. Between 1923 and 1931 she won the U.S. women's title seven times.

Playing in a white eyeshade, intent and expressionless, she destroyed her opponents with machine-like precision. They called her "Little Poker Face"; and when Suzanne Lenglen retired, Helen became the new ruler of women's tennis. Only in 1926 when Helen was ill, could Molla Mallory recapture the U.S. championship one last time.

Helen Wills' greatest rival would be another Helen, Helen Hull Jacobs. Jacobs became Forest Hills champion in 1932, when the older Helen did not play. The following season, the two Helens met in an epic contest. Jacobs won the first set, 8-6; but the older champion took the second, 6-3. In the next set, Helen Wills began to feel dizzy. The younger woman broke her service twice and took a 3-0 lead, and at that, Helen Wills defaulted.

She went into retirement until 1935, when she met Jacobs at Wimbledon and defeated her. In 1938, she repeated her triumph against the other Helen for an unprecedented eighth Wimbledon win. Then she retired, the undisputed Empress of Tennis.

Don's Grand Slam

In the 1930's a new breed of tennis player appeared in America. For the first time, children whose parents were not rich were able to learn to play tennis on public courts. One such boy was Don Budge, the skinny, red-headed son of a California laundry manager.

Budge had a perfect forehand stroke, but his most famous weapon was his backhand — one of the most powerful ever seen. In 1937 he helped the U.S. team win the Davis Cup for the first time in 10 years. Then he won both Wimbledon and Forest Hills by defeating the great German champion, Baron Gottfried von Cramm.

In 1938, when Budge was 23, he resolved to become the first man to win the Grand Slam of tennis — the Australian, French, British, and American titles. The Aussie match, famed as a killer, was played in temperatures over 100 degrees. Budge triumphed without losing a single set.

In France, Don suffered from stomach trouble and did not play his best. Nevertheless, he won the title after dropping only two sets. Then came Wimbledon — another clean sweep!

Only Forest Hills remained. There Don faced his friend, Gene Mako, who managed to wrest a single set from the Magnificent Redhead in a hard-fought battle. In the end, however, it was Budge — 6-3, 6-8, 6-2, 6-1. He had become the first player ever to win the Grand Slam.

After that, Don Budge turned pro. He could not afford to remain an amateur, and so his talents were lost to Forest Hills.

O That Bobby Riggs!

In those days, it was unthinkable that anyone who played for *money* should enter the great tournaments. Tennis was, after all, a game for gentlefolk!

Players from humble backgrounds found this hard to swallow. They longed for the prestige of the big matches, yet had to settle for the less-favored life

of a tennis pro in order to make ends meet.

One man who was especially bitter about the rules for tennis amateurs was Robert L. Riggs. Raised in modest circumstances, he had the instincts of a natural hustler combined with splendid tennis skills. In 1939, he won both Wimbledon and Forest Hills. He made some money by betting on himself but planned for greater things. First, he would become a great amateur champ. Then he would turn pro and rake in wealth!

Unfortunately, Bobby Riggs lost at Forest Hills in 1940, and Wimbledon was cancelled because of the war. But in 1941, Bobby won his second Forest Hills championship and was ready to launch his dream.

That was in September, 1941. Three months later America was at war, and Riggs' dream was postponed. Afterward, he did become a tennis pro, but great wealth stayed out of reach until many years later.

In 1973 Bobby, ever the hustler, decided to exploit the women's lib movement in tennis. He challenged and beat Margaret Court, a top player. Then he challenged Billie Jean King, amid great publicity. Bobby Riggs played King and lost; but in losing he gained fame and fortune, the two things that had eluded him so long.

Bobby Riggs (right) plays Fred Schroeder in the 1941 semi-finals at Forest Hills, a contest which Riggs won. Schroeder became men's singles champion in 1942.

Riggs was famed as one of the brainest court stars. Here he returns the ball to Frank Kovacs during the 1942 Pro Tennis Championships. Kovacs had been runner-up to Riggs in the 1941 Forest Hills finals.

Riggs (left) beat John Faunce in a 1946 pro match. Early pro tennis players did not earn large amounts of money, and it was considered something of a disgrace to turn pro. The snobbish overtones of tennis as a game for "ladies and gentlemen" have disappeared only in recent years.

Billie Jean King, the most famous pupil of Alice Marble, annoyed the old champion with her self-centered attitude. Marble would later dismiss young Billie Jean because the girl declared that some day she would be the best tennis player ever seen. Marble had her own idea of who was greatest!

Alice in Tennisland

Once there was a blonde, pretty girl named Alice Marble. She played a powerful game of tennis, similar to that of a man; and by the time she was 20, she was ranked Number 2 in the United States.

The following year, 1933, Alice suffered a disaster. She was entered in both a singles and a doubles tournament and because of rain, had to play both the semi-finals and the finals of both contests on a single day. The temperature was above 100 degrees; and when Alice finished (without winning), she collapsed. Her fatigue led to tuberculosis, and it seemed as though her tennis career might be over; but she fought back valiantly and made a full recovery by 1936.

That year, she captured the U.S. crown from Helen Jacobs. After a slump in 1937, she won Forest Hills three more times in a row before retiring to do war work during World War II.

Alice Marble brought a new fire to women's tennis, which had been dominated by baseline players for years. Marble was a net-rusher and a ball-walloper. She played in sensible shorts — a great innovation in those days — and featured a splendid serve that yielded a good crop of aces.

Alice Marble became the coach of young Billie Jean Moffitt, who would later become the most famous woman champion of all time. Both players had a similar style, a relentless attack that banished the last vestige of "ladylike behavior" from the tennis court.

Pancho on the Prowl

Don Budge and Bobby Riggs had both come from modest backgrounds. The first genuine "poor man's tennis champ" was Pancho Gonzales. His father was a Mexican-American housepainter in Los Angeles, and the family had no money to waste on luxuries such as tennis.

Nevertheless, young Richard Gonzales learned to play the game at a public playground. He had the grace of a panther and a rocket-like service. He loved tennis so much that he dropped out of school so he could play more. Tennis officials banned him from Junior tournaments because of this, so Pancho joined the Navy. When he completed his service, he was reinstated.

Proud, rebellious, outspoken, Pancho Gonzales came to Forest Hills in 1948 already known as an anti-hero. Tennis snobs watched in horror as the talented upstart won the American championship.

The following year, after sounding off angrily on what he considered hypocrisy in amateur tennis, Pancho came back to Forest Hills. The tennis establishment fielded its best man, Wimbledon winner Fred Schroeder. Pancho beat him — 16-18, 2-6, 6-1, 6-2, 6-4.

Then he turned pro.

In the years that followed, the hot-tempered Latin would go from rags to riches on the pro circuit. Playing well into his 40's, he later became coach of the U.S. Davis Cup team and helped young Arthur Ashe to develop into a champion.

Little Mo, Tennis Immortal

They called her "Little Mo" although she was 5 feet 4 inches tall. She appeared smaller out on the court and made her first appearance at Forest Hills when she was only 14 years old in 1949.

Frizzy-haired, with a charming, homely face, she was a cool hand despite her youth. She bowed in the second round. Two years later she was back with her skills greatly improved, and this time she reached the finals.

The 16-year-old Little Mo was the darling of the gallery, the first female player in many years to have the magic spark of stardom. In the finals she met Shirley Fry, the Wimbledon runner-up, and defeated her 6-3, 1-6, 6-4. It was a nerve-wracking contest; and when Maureen won, she let out a howl of triumph and threw her racket high into the air.

As Forest Hills champion for 1951, she was the youngest woman title-holder since May Sutton in 1904. May was 10 weeks younger than Maureen when she won the U.S. women's singles.

In 1952, Little Mo won both Wimbledon and Forest Hills. Her style was cool and deadly accurate, more like that of a mature woman than of a girl. The contrast between her lovable, childlike personality and her killer instinct on the court caught the fancy of the tennis world. Little Mo became the best-loved of all woman champions.

In 1953 she became the first woman to win the Grand Slam, taking the Australian, French, British, and American titles. She was hailed as the greatest female tennis player in history even though she was still so young that there must have been room for improvement.

In 1954, she won the Italian title and then took Wimbledon for the third time in a row. Her future seemed limitless until she took a fateful horseback ride.

A noisy truck startled her horse, which had been a gift from the people of her hometown, San Diego. The frightened animal smashed Maureen's right leg against the side of the truck and threw her into a ditch. At first, it seemed that her injury was not too serious; but as weeks went by, the leg refused to heal properly. Maureen Connolly, triple champion of the United States and Wimbledon, was finished in tennis. She was only 19 years old.

Little Mo became a coaching professional and married Norman Brinker. Her interest in tennis continued throughout the rest of her tragically short life, until she died of cancer at the age of 34. Experts have compared her style with that of Lenglen, Wills, King, and Court. Most of them have concluded that if Maureen Connolly had matured as a tennis player, she would have been the greatest of them all.

Maureen Connolly (right) demolishes England's Jean Quertier on the way to the 1951 U.S. Championship.

Althea Crosses the Line

Tennis was fast losing its image as a game for rich people. Another barrier remained, however. No black players were allowed to compete in the American tournaments that led to seeding at Forest Hills.

Alice Marble was among the many who protested this injustice. The tennis establishment, though, declared blandly that there *was* no color line; the absence of black players was explained by the lack of talent among those who did apply for the tourneys.

Then a player appeared who could not easily be dismissed. Althea Gibson had grown up on the streets of Harlem in New York City. A magnificent natural athlete, she was trained to play tennis by a Virginia physician, Dr. Robert Walter Johnson.

Encouraged by Alice Marble, Althea applied to enter two tournaments. One refused her, but she was accepted by the second. The color line in tennis had been crossed. In 1950 she played at Forest Hills for the first time and put on a good show against the Wimbledon champ, Louise Brough, before bowing.

By 1957, Althea Gibson was a seasoned veteran. She won the women's singles at Wimbledon in July. In August, she became the first Negro to play on the U.S. Wightman Cup team. Then she faced Louise Brough at Forest Hills for the U.S. championship and won.

Althea Gibson won both Wimbledon and Forest Hills the next season as well. Then she turned pro and was shut out of the great tournaments.

Ashe's First Triumphs

Tennis coaches are the unsung heroes of the game. They are the ones who can spot the spark of greatness in an awkward youngster that sets a potential champion apart from merely "good" players. A talented coach, like a talented gardener, nurtures his pupil, disciplines, trains, and hopes for a glorious flowering.

The amateur coaches who have produced champions are very rare. But one man, Dr. Robert Walter Johnson, helped to develop two of them!

A black physician in Virginia, Dr. Johnson loved tennis and helped children to study the game. Each summer, talented black youngsters would come to his house and study under his direction. Dr. Johnson's first star pupil was Althea Gibson. His second was a small, skinny lad named Arthur Ashe, who first came to the doctor's tennis clinic at the age of 10.

At first, Arthur played pretty badly; but he had a certain knack that attracted Johnson and kept him interested. Summer after summer, Arthur Ashe came to Johnson's clinic. He improved so much that the doctor tried to enter Arthur in major Junior tournaments of the U.S. Lawn Tennis Association. Officials refused, but Johnson kept on trying.

In 1960, Arthur Ashe went to St. Louis, where he was able to perfect his skills by playing all winter on an indoor court. He won the USLTA Junior Singles Indoor Tournament and caused a sensation in the tennis world. Graduating from high school, he went

Arthur Ashe in 1975.

Tom Okker of the Netherlands was Arthur Ashe's opponent in the 1968 singles final at Forest Hills.

to college at UCLA, where he starred on the tennis team.

Now Arthur Ashe was too good for the tennis establishment to ignore. He played at Wimbledon in 1963 and also won the U.S. Clay Court title. He helped the American Davis Cup team to win. The following year he won the Eastern Grass Court Championships; and for the first time, he was invited to play at Forest Hills. He made it to the quarter-finals and also received the William M. Johnston Award for sportsmanship.

Arthur was now coached by the great Pancho Gonzales. Each year he played better. He served in the Army, but was allowed plenty of time for tennis.

In 1968 tennis witnessed an amazing change. Both professionals *and* amateurs were to be allowed to compete at Wimbledon and Forest Hills! At Wimbledon, Arthur lost in the semis to Rod Laver; but he won the U.S. Amateur Championship.

Then he went to Forest Hills for the first U.S. Open Tennis Championship. There he faced the best pros and amateurs of the world.

He battled all the way to the finals (passing gallant old Pancho Gonzales on the way), and faced semi-pro Tom Okker of the Netherlands. Their contest was a trade-off until the fifth set when Arthur shot down the "Flying Dutchman" and won the match and the championship.

He had triumphed over the best of the amateurs and the best of the pros. He was the best and proud of it.

Arthur Ashe won the Wimbledon singles title in
1975, upsetting Jimmy Connors.

King becomes Queen

In the late summer of 1959, a plump, teen-age girl in eyeglasses came to play at Forest Hills for the first time. Her name was Billie Jean Moffitt. She had been coached by Alice Marble after learning fundamentals from Clyde Walker at a public park in Long Beach, California.

Billie Jean wasn't too impressed with Forest Hills. The officials seemed pompous to her, and the place was really a private club where the public wasn't welcome. Billie Jean's father was a fireman, and she was quick to resent any hint of snobbishness. Feeling rebellious and uncomfortable, she lost her first match. She lost in the following years, too, when Forest Hills was dominated by Australia's Margaret Smith and graceful Maria Bueno of Brazil.

In 1961, Billie Jean and her friend, Karen Hantze, won the women's doubles title at Wimbledon. Then her career took wild ups and downs. She might have faded away if she had not studied under a brilliant Australian coach, Mervyn Rose, who rebuilt her forehand and taught her how to *think* on the court.

When Billie Jean came to Forest Hills in 1965, she advanced all the way to the finals. There she lost to Margaret Smith.

She was not dismayed, however. She felt in her heart that if she tried hard enough, she could beat Smith and any other woman in the world as well.

She married Larry King, who encouraged her in her tennis career. In 1966, she went to Wimbledon

Billie Jean King holds the U.S. Women's Singles
Trophy. She won in 1967, 1971, 1972, and 1974.

The style of King is similar to that of her early coach, Alice Marble. Both women rushed the net aggressively and were said to "play like men."

Scars from two operations mark King's knees.
More than any other tennis player, she caused
the general public to take an interest in the pro
game.

Australian tennis star Evonne Goolagong poses
with King at Forest Hills after being defeated in
the 1974 finals. Goolagong was 1971 Wimbledon champion.

and won a tough match against Maria Bueno, taking the title. As Wimbledon champion, Billie Jean King felt she had the right to speak her mind about tennis. She declared that amateur tennis was a dying sport and pointed to half-empty galleries at Forest Hills to prove the point.

"All the best players turn pro," Billie Jean said, "and the best of the amateurs have to take money under the table in order to play in the tournaments. Tennis should be open! Pros and amateurs should be able to play in the big tournaments!"

Her ideas were shocking to U.S. tennis officials in 1966. They told her to stop speaking out, but she refused. The following year, Billie Jean King won both Wimbledon and Forest Hills. She was voted outstanding woman athlete of the world.

She kept on rebelling. Other tennis groups outside the United States agreed with her stand. Open tennis came to stay when Wimbledon allowed pros to compete. The United States was forced to follow suit.

Billie Jean King turned pro. She won the U.S. Open Tennis Championship in 1971, 1972, and 1974 and won at Wimbledon three more times as well. She became a champion of women's rights, especially the right of women athletes to earn as much money as men. She beat Bobby Riggs in the most famous tennis match ever played.

Billie Jean King attracted people to tennis as no other player had ever done before. It was largely because of her that tennis became a popular spectator sport in the United States. She brought back the fans.

Jimbo the Terrible

He came out of Belleville, Illinois, with his best tennis shot a sizzling return of service. But he was far from a budding champ. Young James Scott Connors had been well-taught by his mother, Gloria; but she had not managed to make him great.

"Jimmy," she said, "we'll have to take you to California. My old friend, Pancho Segura, will help you."

Segura, originally from Ecuador, had been U.S. clay court and indoor champion during the 1940's. He helped Jimmy learn to volley and serve and taught him strategy. The boy played at the Beverly Hills Tennis Club with the children of movie stars. He learned a cocky self-assurance and a breezy show-biz manner that would get him into trouble later on.

In 1971, Jimmy Connors won the NCAA title. He reached the finals of six other tournaments but lost them all (the last to 42-year-old Pancho Gonzales). He decided he was good enough to turn pro, and did. It was then that he began to do things that annoyed other players and made him one of tennis' most controversial stars.

"Jimbo" Connors liked to fool around on the court. He was inconsiderate of other people's feelings and hot-tempered when little things got in his way. On the other hand, he went to Wimbledon in 1972 and did very well. He also became the boy friend of lovely young Chris Evert. Romantic tennis fans sighed happily, while hard-working pros gritted their teeth.

Left-handed Jimmy Connors did not attract too much attention until he became Chris Evert's boy friend. He resented playing in her shadow.

Connors pours on the power in a two-handed
backhand.

Manuel Orantes of Spain defeated Connors in the 1975 finals at Forest Hills.

The romance of Jimmy Connors and Chris Evert
foundered when she decided her career was
too important to her to be given up.

Jimmy kept goofing around; but he kept winning tournaments, too. Stardom came in the summer of 1974, when both Jimbo and his fiancee, Chris Evert, won the Wimbledon singles titles.

It was called "the Love Match." A lot of top tennis people, however, disliked Jimmy because he had refused to play for the U.S. Davis Cup team and would not join the players' union.

Jimbo the Terrible came to Forest Hills in 1974, seeded Number 1. Brash Connors had to fight his way to the finals. There he met 39-year-old Ken Rosewall of Australia, who had won at Forest Hills in 1956, when Jimmy was 4!

Their encounter was a rout. Jimmy crushed the veteran from Down Under, 6-1, 6-0, 6-1. It was the most one-sided victory in Forest Hills history.

The engagement of Jimmy and Chris Evert was called off, then called on, then postponed again. Meanwhile, the two young players ruled American tennis as First Seeds.

In 1975, the surface at Forest Hills was changed from grass to Har-Tru, a claylike material. Jimmy still progressed to the finals, losing only one set on the way. In the finale, however, he was defeated, 6-4, 6-3, 6-3, by Spain's Manuel Orantes.

Cocky Jimbo didn't let it get him down. He was only 23 years old, and there would be lots of other championship matches to play.

Chrissie on the Clay

They called her the "Ice Princess," the coolest woman player since "Little Miss Poker Face," the immortal Helen Wills.

Christine Marie Evert of Fort Lauderdale, Florida, learned tennis from her father, Jim. (Years ago, Jim Evert had played on tour with Jimmy Connors' mother!) Six-year-old Chris played with never a smile. Tennis was serious business to her, even when she was very young.

Because her backhand was weak, her father taught her to use a two-handed grip. Her best game was played from the baseline in classic style. Not for her the net-rushing fireworks of Billie Jean King! What she lacked in sparkle, though, she made up for in talent. Chris Evert was a winner.

In 1970, when she was only 15, she managed to defeat Wimbledon champ, Margaret Smith Court, in a tournament held in North Carolina. The following spring, she beat Billie Jean King in the Virginia Slims Masters.

She was selected for the Wightman Cup team in 1971, the youngest player since Maureen Connolly. In the last round of the Wightman, it was Chris Evert who won the trophy for the United States.

That fall, she was the talk of Forest Hills. This tournament, though, was played on grass, which was not Chris's favorite surface. She had learned to play on clay, and it was there that she was at her best. Despite the technical problem, Chris advanced to the semi-finals, where she gave Billie Jean King

In 1971, 16-year-old Chris Evert won the
quarter-finals at Forest Hills by defeating Lesley
Hunt. A grim expression and a grunt as she
swung became her trademarks.

As Billie Jean King retires from the tennis scene, Chris Evert hopes to become America's new Queen of Tennis.

the scare of her life before bowing, 6-3, 6-2.

As Chris became better and better, tennis fans looked toward her as the game's next woman superstar. She won many a tournament but never even got to the finals at Forest Hills. It was the fault of the grass!

In 1972, Chris lost to Evonne Goolagong at Wimbledon. Revenge came a month later, when Chris beat Evonne for her first U.S. Clay Courts title. She would win this championship so often and so easily that people would say she "owned" it!

Then came 1974, her best year yet. She won the French, Italian, and Canadian Open championships. And she won Wimbledon. On the grass! She went to Forest Hills full of hope, but Goolagong wiped her out in the semi-finals.

The following year, Forest Hills officials decided to change the surface of the championship courts. A hard surface called Har-Tru, similar to clay, was laid down. Chris had won 83 straight matches on clay. She was a heavy favorite to win.

This year, she reached the Forest finals for the first time. In the crucial match, she faced Evonne Goolagong.

The catlike Australian won the first set, 7-5. Grimly, Chris hit harder, pressing Goolagong at every chance. Chris won the second set, 6-4. In the third, Chris pressed her advantage and distracted Evonne with her baseline game. The Australian weakened, and Chris won set and match, 6-2. She was U.S. champion at last.

"That's better!" said Chris Evert with a smile. "Wimbledon was great, but this is home!"

U.S. Tennis Champions at Forest Hills

WOMEN'S SINGLES		MEN'S SINGLES	
	U. S. Lawn Tennis Association Championships		
1915	Molla Bjurstedt	1915	William M. Johnston
1916	Molla Bjurstedt	1916	R. N. Williams
1917	Molla Bjurstedt	1917	R. L. Murray
1918	Molla Bjurstedt	1918	R. L. Murray
1919	Hazel Hotchkiss Wightman	1919	William M. Johnston

1920	Molla Bjurstedt Mallory	1920	Bill Tilden
1921	Molla Bjurstedt Mallory	1921	Bill Tilden
1922	Molla Bjurstedt Mallory	1922	Bill Tilden
1923	Helen Wills	1923	Bill Tilden
1924	Helen Wills	1924	Bill Tilden
1925	Helen Wills	1925	Bill Tilden
1926	Molla Bjurstedt Mallory	1926	René Lacoste
1927	Helen Wills	1927	René Lacoste
1928	Helen Wills	1928	Henri Cochet
1929	Helen Wills	1929	Bill Tilden
1930	Betty Nuthall	1930	John Doeg
1931	Helen Wills Moody	1931	Ellsworth Vines
1932	Helen Jacobs	1932	Ellsworth Vines
1933	Helen Jacobs	1933	Fred Perry
1934	Helen Jacobs	1934	Fred Perry
1935	Helen Jacobs	1935	Wilmer Allison
1936	Alice Marble	1936	Fred Perry
1937	Anita Lizana	1937	Don Budge
1938	Alice Marble	1938	Don Budge
1939	Alice Marble	1939	Bobby Riggs
1940	Alice Marble	1940	Don McNeill
1941	Sarah Palfrey Cooke	1941	Bobby Riggs
1942	Pauline Betz	1942	Fred Schroeder
1943	Pauline Betz	1943	Joseph R. Hunt
1944	Pauline Betz	1944	Frank Parker
1945	Sarah Palfrey Cooke	1945	Frank Parker
1946	Pauline Betz	1946	Jack Kramer
1947	Louise Brough	1947	Jack Kramer
1948	Margaret Osborne du Pont	1948	Pancho Gonzales
1949	Margaret Osborne du Pont	1949	Pancho Gonzales
1950	Margaret Osborne du Pont	1950	Art Larsen
1951	Maureen Connolly	1951	Frank Sedgman
1952	Maureen Connolly	1952	Frank Sedgman
1953	Maureen Connolly	1953	Tony Trabert
1954	Doris Hart	1954	Vic Seixas
1955	Doris Hart	1955	Tony Trabert
1956	Shirley J. Fry	1956	Ken Rosewall
1957	Althea Gibson	1957	Malcolm Anderson
1958	Althea Gibson	1958	Ashley Cooper
1959	Maria Bueno	1959	Neale Fraser
1960	Darlene Hard	1960	Neale Fraser
1961	Darlene Hard	1961	Roy Emerson
1962	Margaret Smith	1962	Rod Laver
1963	Maria Bueno	1963	Rafael Osuna
1964	Maria Bueno	1964	Roy Emerson
1965	Margaret Smith	1965	Manuel Santana
1966	Maria Bueno	1966	Fred Stolle
1967	Billie Jean King	1967	John Newcombe
1968	Margaret Smith Court	1968	Arthur Ashe
1969	Margaret Smith Court	1969	Stan Smith

U. S. Open Tennis Championships

1968	Virginia Wade	1968	Arthur Ashe
1969	Margaret Smith Court	1969	Rod Laver
1970	Margaret Smith Court	1970	Ken Rosewall
1971	Billie Jean King	1971	Stan Smith
1972	Billie Jean King	1972	Ilie Nastase
1973	Margaret Smith Court	1973	John Newcombe
1974	Billie Jean King	1974	Jimmy Connors
1975	Chris Evert	1975	Manuel Orantes

SPORTS CLASSICS

WORLD SERIES
U.S. OPEN GOLF CHAMPIONSHIP
WIMBLEDON TENNIS TOURNAMENT
KENTUCKY DERBY
INDIANAPOLIS 500
OLYMPIC GAMES
SUPER BOWL
MASTERS TOURNAMENT OF GOLF
STANLEY CUP
NBA PLAY-OFFS
ROSE BOWL
AMERICA'S CUP YACHT RACE
WINTER OLYMPICS
PGA CHAMPIONSHIP TOURNAMENT
TRIPLE CROWN
AMERICAN TENNIS CHAMPIONSHIP
DAYTONA 500
GRAND PRIX
BOXING'S HEAVYWEIGHT CHAMPIONSHIP

CREATIVE EDUCATION